SAN FRANCISCO EARTHQUAKE

Published by Abdo & Daughters, 6537 Cecilia Circle, Bloomington, Minnesota 55435

Library bound edition distributed by Rockbottom Books, Pentagon Tower, P.O. Box 36036, Minneapolis, Minnesota 55435

Library of Congress Number: 88-71723   ISBN: 0-939179-43-1

Cover Photo by:
Inside Photos by:
     Bettmann Archive: pg. 1, 5, 10, 18, 20, 22, 25, 28, 31
     Underwood Photo Archives: pg. 9, 15

The Day of the Disaster

SAN FRANCISCO EARTHQUAKE

April 18, 1906

Written By: Sue L. Hamilton
Edited By: John C. Hamilton

NOTE: The following is a fictional account based on factual data.

SAN FRANCISCO EARTHQUAKE

APRIL 18, 1906
10:00 a.m.
"As I stood there, the street suddenly began to roll up and down, like a wave on an ocean, until the road crumbled into pieces. From above, homes and businesses exploded. Wood, glass, brick, and plaster rained down. I was afraid I'd be swallowed by the ground or buried alive under the rubble. I wasn't alone. From the early-morning silence, the street came alive with the terrified screams of people. Frightened people. Hurt people. People lost. People dying."

The quiet of an early Wednesday morning is shattered by a low rumbling that grows into the thunderous roar of a devastating earthquake. The quake lasts only a minute, but in that time the entire city of San Francisco will change. From the richest homes to the smallest shacks, businesses, sky-scrapers, roads — the quake misses nothing.

And even after the ground stops shaking, huge fires spread through the city. People will lose everything: their homes, their belongings, their money, even their lives. This is one policeman's story of that disastrous day when San Francisco crumbled under nature's uncontrollable fury.

FORWARD — NEARLY A CENTURY OF THE SHAKES

JUNE 21 - JULY 17, 1808
San Francisco's Presidio (military fort) is hit with some 20 earthquakes. The quakes easily turn many sun-baked clay buildings into mounds of dust.

JUNE 10, 1836   7:30 a.m.
Terrified citizens try to escape as fissures (cracks) open in the ground all the way along the East San Francisco Bay area.

MAY 15, 1851   8:00 a.m.
San Franciscans begin their morning with a medium-sized earthquake. Plaster drops from ceilings and dishes fall from shelves. Several homes and businesses are destroyed.

NOVEMBER 22, 1852   11:52 a.m.
Ten miles southwest of San Francisco, a quake causes cracks in the ground so deep that the water in nearby Lake Merced drains through the cracks into the Pacific Ocean.

JANUARY 9, 1857
Commonly known as the "Fort Tejon Earthquake," this is the strongest quake to hit in the recorded history of the area. The quake is felt along the entire length and width of California. For San Franciscans, it strikes suddenly in the early morning hours; buildings lurch and sway, tossing sleeping townspeople from their beds.

Fort Tejon, an army post under construction at Tejon Pass in the Tehachapi Mountains, is totally destroyed, forcing many soldiers out into the life-threatening cold.

7

In Los Angeles and the surrounding area, homes sway and crumble. Reports from the San Fernando Valley indicate that the ground was moving so quickly and rapidly that it was nearly impossible to stay standing up.

In all, the quake traveled some 275 miles along the California coast, following the course of what is now known as the famous San Andreas Fault, wrecking and destroying everything in its path.

MARCH 5, 1864
Windows shatter, sending sharp pieces of glass shooting from businesses and homes, as a "mild" quake rolls through San Francisco.

OCTOBER 8, 1865   12:07 p.m.
Everyday activities halt as a powerful earthquake rocks San Francisco. A fissure two blocks long cracks Howard Street in half, stopping traffic. The road must be leveled and totally rebuilt.

OCTOBER 21, 1868   12:01 p.m.
The death toll reaches 30 as a major earthquake strikes San Francisco on this calm Sunday afternoon.

With the ground rolling and buildings collapsing, people and horses alike race terrified through the streets seeking the safety of an open area. The ground moves like waves on the ocean, giving people the queasy stomachs usually associated with sea sickness.

POLICEMAN'S DIARY

MONDAY, APRIL 16, 1906
6:00 a.m.

I just finished my first night on the job. The boys at the station house were teasing me about never having felt an earthquake. Well, I'm ready whenever old Mother Nature wants to shake things up a bit! It can't be worse than some of the tornadoes that rip through my home town in Kansas.

This city is one of the strangest places I've ever seen. Why, tonight when I was on duty, I had to break up a prayer meeting! The preacher was yelling and screaming that the sinners of the city would pay for all their wrong-doings, that God would come and destroy everything. Maybe so, but not today.

TUESDAY, APRIL 17, 1906
6:30 a.m.

That same preacher was at it again tonight! This time I ran him in for disturbing the peace. I won't have to deal with him for the rest of the week.

WEDNESDAY, APRIL 18, 1906
5:00 a.m.

It's been an unusually quiet night on the streets. Almost too quiet . . . I'm taking a few moments to write while my horse rests. He's been nervous and uneasy all evening, as if he knows that something is about to happen. If only he could tell me what. It seems strange. I feel as if something big is about to happen. I hope whatever it is, it happens on someone else's shift.

5:13 a.m.
What's that rumbling noise? The ground is shaking! An earthquake! I can't stand up . . .

5:14 a.m.
The shaking has stopped. But for how long? This is unbelievable! That preacher was right! The city is in ruins! It looks as though it's been bombed. People are screaming, terrified. I've got to help them . . .

10:00 a.m.
I'm still alive. San Francisco is a disaster area. From the new $7 million city hall to the slum hotels in the ghetto, the destruction is everywhere. It all happened so fast, and yet it felt as though it would never stop. Less than a minute passed, but what a minute!

As I stood there, the street suddenly began to roll up and down, like a wave on an ocean, until the road crumbled into pieces. From above, homes and businesses exploded. Wood, glass, brick, and plaster rained down. I was afraid I'd be swallowed by the ground or buried alive under the rubble.

12

I wasn't alone. From the early-morning silence, the street came alive with the terrified screams of people. Frightened people. Hurt people. People lost. People dying.

The noise was deafening: People and animals yelling and crying. The quake rumbling. The screech of metal twisting, buildings crumbling, windows shattering, chimneys falling. The roar became unbearable.

And then it stopped. For a second after the quake ended, everyone and everything seemed to pause and wait and listen . . . Then came the shouts and screams, the confusion, the reality that all that had been there seconds ago was now gone or changed.

General Funston, in charge at the Presidio, has placed the city under his command. The army, police, and fire department are working together to keep things under control.

We're under orders to shoot looters. However, there have already been some tragic mistakes because of this policy. Several people have been shot who seemed to be looting, but were, in fact, going through the remains of their own homes, trying to save what few possessions they could. I refuse to shoot anyone until I know for sure that person is stealing. If you call out to someone and he turns and runs away, it's pretty easy to figure out that he's doing something wrong. Unfortunately, most of the soldiers don't care to take the time to do this. They shoot first, ask questions later.

Overall, though, the people have been wonderful. One would expect complete panic, but after the first few minutes, everyone began helping each other. San Francisco may be destroyed, but its people are stronger and better than ever.

Speaking of people, one of the strangest moments I had today was while standing in front of the Palace Hotel. Its big glass dome had shattered and crumbled. People, many cut from the pieces of glass, walked aimlessly, crying, when suddenly from one of the windows above came the voice of the opera singer Caruso. Everyone stopped to listen. Somehow, it was reassuring to hear his

14

strong, clear voice breaking through the fear and confusion. Hard to believe, but it took an earthquake for me to hear my first opera!

Afterward, Caruso left the hotel to go to the docks. Apparently his manager thought it'd be safer for him on a boat. Of course, if another quake strikes under the water in the bay, it could cause a tsunami, or giant wave, that can easily sink a large ship. Unlike a tornado, where one can seek safety in a cellar or basement, there's no true safe place from an earthquake.

Right now the city is quiet again. Nothing is working. No lights. No heating gas. No telephone or telegraphs. No running water. And worst of all, the sewer pipes are broken — no toilets!

With no water, no toilets, and many dead still lying in the streets, the smell is horrible. People can live with smells, but it's nearly impossible to live through a case of typhoid fever, a disease that all these "no's" add up to.

Typhoid — the mere mention of the word terrifies me. I've seen it before, after a tornado swept

16

through my home town. People get it from eating or drinking rotten food or water. Victims experience burning fevers, rashes, and bleeding inside the body — a painful, awful way to die. We are warning people to be very careful; to boil all their drinking water and to eat only canned goods. Still, many are sure to die.

On this sad thought, I'm going to sleep a couple hours. I'm too tired to think or move any more.

1:00 p.m.
Fire! I thought the worst was over — it's only begun! I just woke up, and I've been assigned to help with one of the three big fires that broke out in the city. Broken gas pipes, dry wooden buildings, and no water have added up to yet another disaster.

San Francisco was built with buildings close together; there are no open spaces that can stop the fire from spreading. The flames simply reach across the road to the next building and it starts burning. There's *still* no running water!

Raging fire over the city of San Francisco.

18

6:00 p.m.

I saw my friend the preacher up on his church trying to beat out the flames that had reached the roof. It was an impossible task, for in less than five minutes, the entire church was in flames — he was barely able to leap to safety.

Even as night falls, the city is lit up like day. The firefighters are doing everything to stop the flames, but without water the three fires have now come together into one giant inferno. It's unstoppable. San Francisco is burning.

The only thing left to do is to bring in as much dynamite as possible, and try to blast down buildings to open up enough space so the flames can't leap across.

It's up to us, the police force, to get people out as quickly as possible. All the automobiles owned by citizens have been taken over to help the wounded and sick. That leaves horses. I've heard people trying to buy a horse for a thousand dollars. No one is selling. People have to *walk* out of the city.

It's such a sad sight. Exhausted people trying to carry trunks and cases filled with whatever they have left. But the steep hills of San Francisco don't make it easy to carry much weight very far. With flames hot on their heels, one by one, item-by-item, people are forced to drop their possessions and move on with nothing but the shirts on their backs. The streets are lined with trunk after discarded trunk . . . until the flames reach them, destroying everything.

Still, people must think of saving themselves first. We've got to get them out of the way in order to set off the dynamite.

THURSDAY, APRIL 19, 1906

10:00 a.m.
The *Call, Chronicle,* and *Examiner* newspapers worked together to put out one morning edition. Their headlines: "Earthquake and Fire: San Francisco in Ruins;" "No Hope Left for Safety of Any Buildings;" "Whole City is Ablaze." This'll be the last paper issued for awhile — all three of their buildings have been destroyed by the fire.

3:00 p.m.

We've been fighting fire all day. The regular dynamite is gone. They're using something called "giant powder," a type of dynamite that is starting more fires than stopping them. The soldiers don't even know how to handle this stuff. I've been keeping myself as far away as possible from where they're setting the explosives. I believe the entire city is going to burn.

5:30 p.m.

I thought the city looked as though it'd been bombed right after the quake. Well, now the army has brought in cannons to try to bomb down buildings. Even this hasn't stopped the flames.

FRIDAY, APRIL 20, 1906

10:00 a.m.

The fires have, for the most part, simply burned themselves out. Few buildings have survived. Those that made it through the quake were taken by the fire. Those still standing during the fire were dynamited down. What was left from the dynamite was bombed.

More so than ever, General Funston and Mayor Schmitz are running things. Overall, they are getting things done — seeing that people have food, clothing and some kind of shelter. Tents have been set up all over the city.

The soldiers are still trigger happy. Groups of citizens have put themselves in charge of keeping order in their neighborhoods — they are more dangerous than the thieves. Signs have been posted around town: "Obey Orders or Get Shot!" Luckily, my police uniform seems to give me some power to stop these people when I can.

It's been two days of disaster after disaster. If ever I felt needed in a job, it's been here. San Franciscans have really come together helping each other through the disaster, but now comes the hard part — rebuilding their homes, businesses, and lives from almost nothing.

EPILOGUE —
THE FINAL COST

FRIDAY, MAY 18, 1906
8:00 a.m.
A month has passed since the quake struck. The newspapers have published the results of nature's fury:

- 2,000 people dead, or missing and assumed dead
- 250,000 people left homeless — nearly half the city's population
- 500 city blocks burned to the ground
- 30,000 buildings destroyed (3,000 by fire)
- $500 million total damages

That preacher who I arrested for disturbing the peace blames himself for bringing God's anger onto the city. He's being cared for in a hospital nearby.

I don't really know if God decided to level the city, but San Francisco is being rebuilt with the help and kindness of people across the country. Some $9 million dollars have come in — including $30,000 collected by the police in the city of Chicago.

A famous architect, David Burnham, came up with a big plan to rebuild San Francisco like Paris, France. Well, if you ask me, this isn't Paris, and we don't need all the grand and glorious designs. We need buildings that will withstand the shaking of a quake. We need safety. We need more than one water main. We need a plan to get people out of the city quickly. The citizens of San Francisco must be protected.

Many people have chosen to leave. I figure the worst is over — I'm staying. I've seen the best in people come through in the worst possible conditions. I'll help rebuild and protect. But I'll always remember that minute when the earth moved as though it were alive. April 18, 1906 — a day that will remain forever a day of disaster.

The crew rests in the midst of the devastation as refugees camp in the background.

POSTSCRIPT

1909

Three years later, San Francisco is rebuilt with hundreds of steel-frame buildings designed to withstand the stress of a major quake. A huge new water system is installed to insure that should another major disaster strike, water will be available.

As developers try to get people back into the city to rent and buy newly constructed buildings, they speak of the disaster of 1906 as the "fire" of 1906, not the "earthquake." This angers scientists who are trying to research what causes earthquakes. Andrew Larson, the geologist for whom the San Andreas Fault was eventually named, is forced to keep quiet. Although he eventually founds a national society on earthquake research and writes a huge report on the 1906 quake, the business community is able to keep much of his findings a secret from the rest of the country.

PRESENT DAY

Hundreds of quakes have been recorded since that tragic day back in 1906. However, things are much different today. Research is paid for by the government and the findings published worldwide. Scientists have developed such devices as seismometers and seismographs for detecting and recording earthquakes.

Building materials have been tested. The findings show that during an earthquake, wooden houses can bend with the movement of a quake, as can specially designed concrete-over-steel columns, such as those found in San Francisco's Transamerica Building. Brick and stone buildings tend to crumble. Any survivor of 1906 will recall how dangerous it was when chimneys collapsed into the streets.

Even with all of today's modern equipment and knowledge, earthquakes are still uncontrollable and frightening. We must continue to study each quake and learn from the mistakes and tragedies others have faced.

April 18, 1906: A day in history when nature's power killed hundreds of people and destroyed most of San Francisco. In less than a minute, this day became a day of tragedy. A day of disaster.

SOURCES CONSULTED

Bolt, Bruce A. *Earthquakes.* New York: W.H. Freeman and Company, 1988.

Earthquake History of the United States. Colorado: U.S. Department of Commerce, National Oceanic and Atmospheric Administration and U.S. Department of the Interior, Geological Survey, 1982.

Fisher, Ron; Melham, T.; Ramsay, C.R.; and Stuart, G.S. *Nature On The Rampage: Our Violent Earth.* Washington D.C.: The National Geographic Society, 1986.

London, Jack. "The Story of an Eye-Witness." *Collier's,* May 5, 1906, pp. 22-25.

Palmer, Frederick. "A Stricken City Undismayed." *Collier's,* May 12, 1906, pp. 9-11.

Palmer, Frederick. "San Francisco In Ruins." *Collier's,* May 5, 1906, pp. 12-13.

Ritchie, David E. *Superquake! Why Earthquakes Occur and When the Big One Will Hit Southern California.* New York: Crown Publishers, Inc., 1988.

Walker, Bryce and The Editors of Time-Life Books. *Planet Earth: Earthquake.* Virginia: Time-Life Books, Inc., 1982.